Hospital Poems

Nancy Dunlop

Nancy Dunlop

Indie Blu(e) Publishing
Havertown, Pennsylvania

PRAISE FOR HOSPITAL POEMS

"Harrowing and comforting, this riveting collection is therapeutic by design. As both an inpatient and outpatient of mental hospitals, poet Nancy Dunlop becomes a keen observer: "What we did, mostly/ was watch each other." One patient is "sad. Slumped and furtive." One doctor is "like a job title . . . a perfect/ brochure." In swift, visceral portraits, the poet gives glimpses of the agitated mind's *carnival* as well as the medicated body's *shudder, quiver, spasm. Hospital Poems* opens with agitation and an apparition as a newcomer enacts a seemingly endless loop. The book ends with patience: Two souls in a waiting room offer solace by their shared presence. We watch as each body "holds on for dear life." Readers are entrusted with stories of those who "had already/ suffered, already knew/ how to be compassionate." Dunlop's humanity teaches us to build relationships. Her violent concision cultivates a clarity that helps us navigate trauma with empathy."

—Lori Anderson Moseman, *Okay?*

"In each of these keenly observed poems, Dunlop portrays a person in a unique struggle to survive a mental crisis or the soulless hospital environment. But these are anything but depressing tales. Rather, "Hospital Poems" is a short but deftly sketched set of portraits of people who shine with the light of humanity.

Nancy Dunlop may not [by her own admission] be able to explain how a person turns into a mental patient but she knows exactly how to turn that mental patient back into a person."

—Claudia Ricci, *Sister Mysteries*

"Life gets out of hand. Despair is misunderstood. But there's no loss of — or wasted — words in the bravely written, honest portraits of the co-patients and experience Nancy Dunlop offers up in *Hospital Poems.* Circumstances for these poems bring heightened awareness to her lines and stanzas, grounded in vulnerability and much detail."

—Christopher Funkhouser, *Prehistoric Digital Poetry: An Archaeology of Forms, 1959-1995*

"Nancy Dunlop's *Hospital Poems* is both narrative and teleportative, delivering readers directly into the sparse setting of a psychiatric hospital. This collection of poems is a reflection on one woman's experience with mental and physical illness through the lens of fascinating characters the speaker encounters during a hospital stay. Characters are intriguing, often whimsical, and brimming with personalities that inject the sterile setting with vibrance.

Dunlop transforms a place of confusion, uncertainty, and despair into a place of ethereal wonder, where characters rely on tenacity and empathy to reimagine the world outside hospital walls, while others grapple with the mundanity of life inside.

An emotional journey of self-exploration and acceptance."

—Mel Sherrer, *Vice Grip*

"Some of us — Nancy Dunlop among them — get, despite ourselves, a deep look into & experience of this oh so modern *condition humaine* of depression, psychic breakdown & mental hospital stays. Rare are those who, like her, come back &, without harping on their own grief, report on those met *in situ*. Dunlop knows that "the predators that make me growl are inside me" & that there are "No guarantees. No promises." And yet she is able to offer us clear-eyed & -voiced poems that she gives us *Straight*, with *No* (sugary, self-pitying) *Chaser*, & that, like Monk's composition of that title, could be called "classical blues in B-flat minor.""

—Pierre Joris, *Celebratory Talk-Essay on Receiving the Batty Weber Award*

"If Nancy Dunlop's *Hospital Poems* were a record album it would be a "concept album." Far from merely being a collection of poetry, it has a unity of theme that many collections lack. Dunlop's bravery in creating this deeply personal collection is in evidence before the reader is even done with her introduction...

This is an excellent collection of poetry concerning a subject that still needs to be drug out into the light of day and cured of its stigmata. Nancy Dunlop lays it all out of the pages of this book for everyone to see, these pages are soaked with blood, pain, and hope. Hope and understanding are what one is left with as you turn the last page. It takes a bit of a journey to get there, but it is well worth the ride."

—John W. Leys, *Whispers of a One-Eyed Raven: Mythological Poetry*

"It seems there's not a person left on the planet who doesn't know of someone who has been institutionalized, medicated, DSM diagnosed. Or knows countless others below radar, in crisis but lacking the means or ability to seek medical help, therapy, counseling. What Nancy Dunlop has done, however, is make us aware that this "epidemic" is not something "out there," a contagion belonging to others; to paraphrase her, we are all perpetually writing our way into and out of our own private hospitals. Coping in an age where living so often just seems to get harder, more overwhelming-- sadder--seems increasingly a matter of constantly travelling back and forth on some despair-felicity continuum. The inpatient/outpatient binary is literal in her book, but it offers an emotional metaphor for managing the "hauntings and agitations" so many of us can't help but daily experience in varying degrees. And in having the guts to share her own intimate experiences living on the extreme edges of this continuum, Dunlop's matter-of-fact, crystal clear observations show people in crisis as the regular folk that they are. That we all are. This is more than a poetics of empathy; what Dunlop does is calmly gives us permission to consider sharing, and bringing our own narratives, into the mix."

—Derek Owens, *The Villagers*

For information, address
Indie Blu(e) Publishing
indieblucollective@gmail.com

Paperback ISBN: 978-1-951724-17-7
eBook ISBN: 978-1-951724-19-1
Library of Congress Control Number: 2022941647
Indie Blu(e) Editorial Team
Candice Louisa Daquin
Victoria Manzi
Christine E. Ray
Cover Artwork: Joan Dumouchel

ACKNOWLEDGEMENTS

Many thanks to Christine Ray and Candice Louisa Daquin of Indie Blu(e) for the warmth and sensitivity you showed toward this collection and toward me.

Thank you to Joan Dumouchel for allowing the use of your wonderful painting on the cover.

Thank you to all who offered such eloquent and caring advance reviews. I feel the love.

Thanks, also, to the Howe Memoir Workshop, as well as other friends and associates, for helping to shepherd early drafts of these poems into their final shapes.

And to my fellow patients whose re-imaginings populate these pages, I hope I have done you justice.

DEDICATION

For Stephen

PROLOGUE

How did I become a patient in a mental hospital? Not just once, but over and over?

The answer will disappoint. The answer is, 'I don't really know.' And I don't want to talk about the obvious: the medics, the gurneys, the ambulance lights, a cop or two, a horrified spouse. These are things that are expected. Feared, but at least expected.

No. What I want to talk about is another kind of transit from outside the hospital to in. A mysterious and visceral trip. Like you've been cast into a river separating two shores. But no oarsman transports you. There is no boat. You are not buoyed on top of the water. You are submerged, deep under the black surface. Suspended in a sort of thick, aqueous fluid, shuttled forward slowly in the dark.

There's a good chance you lack any clear thinking and later can't remember details of this nether place. But for those whose lives are interrupted by hospital stays, those thick deep waters exist, and you must pass through them each time in order to change from being a person into a patient.

What is it that 'qualifies' you to stop being a person? To be a mental patient? To be 'sick enough,' 'mad enough,' (do they still say 'mad'?), 'crazy enough' to find yourself inside? What is the medical term? What goes on in those phone conversations between doctors on the outside and doctors on the inside? What are they saying about you?

Throughout the past decade, I have been in and out of mental hospitals at least five times, pretty much annually and pretty much around the same date on the calendar. You can wonder about that date and why. But don't bother asking me. I don't really know.

But if you, like me, are a repeat offender, you might not know the details of how or why you got in, either. How you were forced to leave one shore, cross depths, and awake in a little bed in a dim room to the beep of the monitor by the nurse's station, waiting to check your vitals.

That *Beep Beep Beep* signals that you have once again travelled to the other side. You are now in the hospital. You are now a patient again. With other patients. Who seem so much not like patients, but like people, whose lives got out of hand, whose despair got misunderstood, who were at a loss for words when words were demanded of them.

These poems provide some words, and I hope they help, just a bit, to make these patients into people again. Me included. And maybe you, too.

CONTENTS

INPATIENT

OUTPATIENT

INPATIENT
POEMS

#

A WHITER SHADE OF PALE

She was the first one I saw
when they brought me into the ward.

An apparition gliding toward me,
like she had died and was staying in this place,
moving through the halls in an ivory robe,
coming out to greet newcomers.

I had never seen anyone
so white. Translucent as porcelain, with eyes
set deep in her head, seeming to see things
not of this world. She was both beautiful
and frightening.

She looked the way I felt.
Did I float like her? Did others?

The next morning,
she bounded into the kitchen, showered and
dressed and cheerful. She sat down at the table
and started talking. A lot.

She was anything but dead.

"I had such a bad migraine yesterday.
Have you seen my husband yet?"

She pulled a photo from her pocket,
passed it around.

I took it and looked and there was her husband,
a large man, dark as chocolate,
with a gentle smile, holding
their mocha daughter.

"I loved him so much. He was
shot and killed two days ago.
He was a great father."

I was struck dumb,
watching her mouth move, unable
to take this in.

Who shot him?
Was there a gun loose in the house, on the street?
Did he do it?
Was it a cop?

She went on happily about how
wonderful he was,
reciting the same story
in the same way,
in the same order,
with the same words,
over and over.

Overall, she was very nice.
She was one of the patients who
took up coloring, working
on xeroxed copies
of mandalas, very intricate.

She would sit at a sunny window,
white and luminous as hope, itself,
finishing one mandala, starting another,
asking anyone who passed:
"Have you seen my husband yet?"

SPILLED MILK

Patients were always curious
about newcomers. New arrivals
were an event. We'd huddle in the hall
and gawk at newbies.

So one day,
a new one came in, filled out
forms at the nurses' station. She jerked and spun,
her arms reaching randomly
at the air, like a marionette,
her hands gripping and releasing, her head
stuck solid to one side.

As she walked, she lurched and even
when she was simply waiting her turn
at the meds window, she rocked
side to side. I thought, 'Poor woman. She has
Cerebral Palsy and also needs to be in here
with us, in a mental hospital.' But my Roommate
was older than me, more versed
in such things. She said, "No. It's not Palsy;
It's from the meds."

I was, as yet,
an innocent, listening and learning,
on my bed, back
against the wall, hugging
a pillow.
(No stuffed animals permitted on the ward.)

Would that puppet woman ever be
cured of those eruptions?
Can a hospital help such things? Will she ever
regain the grace inherent
in standing and walking and sitting?

I, too, take drugs strong enough to quell
the wrong things in my head. They make me
shudder from the inside out, quiver
a little bit, spasm my muscles, so
my leg jerks without warning. But only
once in a while. Sometimes, my foot
starts tapping, but I can still
force both feet
on the ground.

Sometimes, my husband quietly signals:
You're touching your mouth again.
I fold my hands in my lap. I can
do this.

Not at all like that woman, her face
wincing, that one morning,
in the kitchen with me and my Roommate. I wanted
to ask her name. But she didn't stay still enough.

She hauled herself up to
get milk for her cereal, not
asking for help, a look in her eyes, like
everything was fine.

When she poured, she spilled
some on the table. My Roommate, who had seen it
all before, and knew far more

about such things, said to this
woman, "Wipe that up."

And wouldn't you know, that lurchy woman
got up, got a towel,
and wiped up her mess.

If it had been me, I would have
cried. But
there seemed to be some sort
of understanding
between these two women,
these veterans. An awareness
of a whole different level, a rung
further down in the pit.

And now, as I try yet another pill,
I sense the quaking within, remembering
that lurchy woman in the hospital,
whose name I never learned.

THE KID

There would always be kids
in the mix of patients. High school,
college-aged, hospitalized
during Spring Break.

Many of them were kind, easy
to sit with, not afraid of talking
with adults. They had already
suffered, already knew
how to be compassionate.

But this one kid: He never
shut up. He knew everything
about everything. He was also
a raging alcoholic. He would
go on and on about
any topic, until someone said,
'Alcoholism,' and he'd be gone
in a shot.

The interesting thing about this kid
was that he read. A lot.
Not many of us were readers. No
attention span. But this kid
not only read, he read
big, fat books. Good ones. A tome
of Kerouac poems. Then onto
another fat book, this one
on Ginsberg.

And he was always
quiet when he read. Off,
by himself. But still,
within range of the rest of us.

One day, I said to him, "You know,
I knew Ginsberg. I can fill you in
on more names you should read if you're
serious about this stuff." He looked up
from his book, nodded, and went
back to his reading.

Days went by. When he wasn't
reading, this kid was driving
people crazy. In a mental hospital.
But really, he was just too much. He knew
what the moderator was going to say
before she said it. He knew about
this technique, that
solution, the danger mark
for high cholesterol, and be careful of
too much flax. He knew all about *Nadi Sodham*,
the ancient art of alternate
nostril breathing, chattering
his way through meditation hour.

One time, in Group, he
interrupted someone. Again. I said,
"Stop interrupting, now. No more talking.
Just listen."

And he did these things.

It was like nobody had ever called him
out. Given him that kind
of attention. The slightest of boundaries.
Like a book in the hand, a front cover, a back
cover, and
you know when to start, when you're finished.
Or like a baby touching either side
of a crib, reassured he won't
fall out.

Shortly after that, he approached me, asked,
"Did you really work with Ginsberg?"
I said, "Yes."

He said, "I'd be interested in
the names of those poets
you mentioned." I said, "Okay."

He asked for a pen. I said,
"Find one." He asked for
some paper. I said, "Get it, yourself."

And he did these things.

Then he sat across from me
at the kitchen table, quietly,
and took down some names.

THE BEST THAT MONEY CAN BUY

He reeked of old money. For the sake
of this poem, let's call him Larry.

Larry would begin his day with a stroll
to the meds window, for morning med call,
his bathrobe, burgundy velvet, belted
with a gold tassel, burnished leather
mules on his feet, his silver hair
sleeked into a little ponytail. So grand compared
to the rest of us, the disheveled ones,
straggling out of our rooms, trailing blankets.

After meds, Larry would retire to his room
for a morning nap, confident
the staff would come back from the dining hall
with his coffee and breakfast prepared
as he requested.

When he at last changed into
his day clothes, he would beeline
to the TV Room, turn on *Law and Order:SVU*,
and sit there, straight-backed and regal,
staring at the screen. Other patients would
come and go, also entranced by *Law and
Order:SVU*.
Everyone, not just Larry, loved that show.

But that is kind of how TV works
in the hospital. One show, over and over, all day.
Before Larry arrived, a young woman,
a kindergarten teacher, in for a round of
shock treatments, dominated the TV room

10

with *The Golden Girls*. When the theme song
started, that sweet
young woman would turn to us, say: "Oh look,
another one."
And she would chuckle at herself.

But Larry didn't chuckle. Larry never
made jokes about Larry. He sat silently,
waiting for the next episode. The next
little chunk of his day.

One time, I got to talk to Larry.
During commercials. We chatted about
television. We debated over whether
Alan Alda was handsome.
We talked (and I don't know how we
got there) about the Weather Underground.

He said he had known Mark Rudd,
one of the FBI's Most Wanted.
Apparently, Larry was also
involved in the student shutdown
of Columbia University during Vietnam.
Who knew he bore such
outlaw mystique?

Soon after Columbia, he said, he got sick.
Did his family
see a problem and send him
to the finest institution money could buy,
getting him out of sight, getting
on with their lives?

His carriage spoke of staid

white sanitariums tucked
in sweeping green hills. A member
of the lineage: Ezra Pound, H.D., Robert Lowell,
Sylvia Plath, James Taylor. One
of the gifted ones. A Mad Genius
communing with the Muse, cavorting
with the Angels, pounding out poem
after masterful poem.

But from Larry... nothing. No
communiqués from the Underground. None
from Heaven, either. What we had here
was a sick man with a trust fund,
in and out of hospitals for the bulk
of his life, watching television, and walking
through corridors, with the confidence
of an aging prince.

KNOCKOUT

She was a Knockout, absolutely
gorgeous. Shining eyes, shining
black hair, ruby plump lips. The jeans
she wore were fierce, torn
just right, in all the right
places, her tank tops just so. And the body
underneath this arrangement: Pow!

All the men followed her around. The women, too,
even the young ones, those lost
souls with way too many piercings,
and too many tattoos, so
medicated, they couldn't
even smile. But Knockout
did it for them. She was the smile.

She was, for all of us,
the key. But not just the key out of the asylum, but
the key
to someplace else. A magical place,
a glass-clinking, chandelier-twinkling party, all of us
in ball gowns instead of bathrobes.

We loved her for that.

Knockout could also be a rebel, a leather-clad
warrior, free
from constraints and petty rules. Life was too short,
she would remind us. Let's just be happy right
this second. Baby, *burn*
that candle! Both ends!

We loved her for that, too.

One morning, she turned
her brights on me, said
she would flat-iron my
frizzy hair. Soon,
I'd be looking great. And for a brief time,
no one in the world mattered but me.

She peered around the corner
to the Nurses' Station,
and when their heads were down, hissed,
"Okay, Now!" and yanked me into her room.

And what a room. A tossed salad of satin dresses,
slick boots, glistening beads, bold
paintings from Arts and Crafts. Red, blue, yellow.
The whole
room pulsed with the very force
of her. Even her roommate, pretty much
unconscious
on her bed, seemed blanketed
in diamonds.

I asked, "Why do you have all these
beautiful things? You're only in here for
a short time." And she hugged a box
she had shellacked with birds, roses, angels, said,
"Because I have nowhere to go. I don't
know where I'll be when I get out of here.
That's how it is. I make home wherever I am."

And then, the kicker. She unrolled the sleeve
of her tee shirt and showed it to me. A...

cigarette! Some of it already smoked.
She held her finger to her lips: *Shhhh…*
and rolled it back into her sleeve.

All this already, and we hadn't even gotten
to my hair. She pulled a flat iron
from under her nightstand, and began her magic.

But like all renegades, the most
beautiful ones, the most determined
shooting stars, eventually they get
brought down. A nurse spotted us, shouted
"Get out of her room!" "Don't touch each other!"
"Step back!"

Knockout protested: "We're just fixing our hair."
And just how little that grain of happy mattered in
that gray,
walled-in world of trite decrees and mediocre
expectations and playing it safe
as a coma.

The flat iron was confiscated. My hair stayed frizzy.
But *Shhhh…*a cigarette still hid
in the fold of a sleeve,
waiting patiently
for a light.

PORTRAIT OF THE ARTIST AS A YOUNG MAN

Newcomers kept to themselves.
This was true of the new guy. But after a while,
he'd appear in the doorway
of the Common Room,
a white wraith, watching us putter about:
chatting or reading or coloring or…
whatever. And that will be his name
for this poem: Whatever.

Whatever was striking. He knew this.
Very tall, thin, aquiline, with tight black jeans
and Euro sneakers. He had, I would discover,
packed a variety of sneakers for
'His Trip to the Hospital.'

Tight black curls straggled over his optic-white
forehead in a casual sort of way, shiny
with 'product.'

Everything about Whatever was
'I'm cool. You're not. I win.'

I first met Whatever in the meditation room.
He was sitting in the electric
massage chair. I said, "Hi, I'm Nancy."
And he said, "Hi Nancy," in the most
whispery soft way, with an odd
soft smile. I thought, *This guy
is really broken.*

One day, Whatever and I
were in the same class. It was called 'How
to Handle Grief.' The moderator
was very good. She had single-handedly lifted
our sorry little group to a place of
actually having some sort
of hope. A momentary respite. Even
some happiness.

That's when Whatever made his move.
His voice came from the far end
of the room, behind the rest of us:

"I had an amazing life. I was
a successful photographer in Manhattan, I had
a giant loft, I had a beautiful
Swedish model girlfriend.
Then I found myself living
under a cardboard box
in San Francisco, so how the FUCK
am I supposed to 'embrace' that?"

It was the way he said, "Fuck,"
that stayed with me. I've heard
a lot of "Fuck's," but this one
rang out. Practiced, sculpted, almost
scripted. His own private *bildungsroman*.

After a while, Whatever
would actually enter the Common Room, sit
by himself, blankly. So one time,
I approached. Sat a little bit away

from him, my hands down, like
approaching a newly
penned pony.

I said, "I was in that group about grief,
and I heard your story, and
I'm sorry." And he
smiled that odd little smile.

He said, "I'm working with Dr. So and So,
and we're talking about electric shock treatment."
I thought back on my time with
Dr. So and So. I said,
"Think carefully before doing that. Think
carefully about that doctor."

And Whatever turned to me, with his
cool blank eyes, his cool black
curls dribbling down his forehead,
and said, in his most whispery voice, "I don't mind
being psychotic."

And I thought, *Fuck you*,
and moved to the far end
of the couch.

THE WOMAN IN THE GREY SWEATER

We wanted to sit with her.
Cultivate her. Get her
to talk. There was something
compelling about her.
Like a fawn that still has its spots,
teetering on newly-born legs.
You wanted her
with you.

We would ask her
to join us at the patio table
when they let us out
because the weather
was so nice, the sun
so bright.

She would approach,
sit down
quietly, smile
shyly. Everything about her
was tender.

Her hair was disheveled
and she wore the same
grey sweater every day.
She would pull at the cuffs,
so that the sleeves
covered her fingertips.

One day, we were talking about
our husbands, our families, those
on the outside, waiting for us
to be released.

The woman in the grey sweater,
pulled at her sleeves and
smiled politely,
without saying a word.

Suddenly, she whispered:
"My husband is a jerk. I'm
afraid for my kids. What he might
do to them."
Then she descended
back into silence, all
the while trying to be polite, to smile
at the right times, or
look concerned, as needed.

That night, it happened.
Just what you think
would happen in a mental hospital.

We saw the orderlies rush
down the hall, the bigger,
burlier ones. We heard the screams.

We looked around to see
who wasn't accounted for.
It was the woman in the grey sweater.

She screamed and screamed,
sounding like a deaf person making
sounds for the first time.

It was all so plaintive. So large
a suffering swelling in wave
after wave, until it was
nothing more than the hollowed
bellowing of a distant sea creature stranded
on some reef, unable to make its way back
into the water.

We huddled together, scared.
Could that have been
any one of us? Was that
why we were in here?

The next morning at breakfast,
they let us sit outside in the sun again.
And the woman came out to join us,
still wearing her grey sweater.
She sat down, smiled quietly at us,
and ate her cereal
without saying a word.

OUTPATIENT POEMS

THE HANDSOME MAN

Once there was a handsome man.
At first, he stayed locked up in the Inpatient Ward.
He slept a lot, in his room at the far end
of the men's hall.

There was so little to do between classes on
Coping Skills like
Five things you see; Four things
you hear; Three things you touch. Or,
Count colors around you: Reds, yellows, blues. Or,
Place your face in a bowl
of ice cubes. And don't forget
how important
exercise is (even though they rarely
took us outside for walks).

And what were we to do between
these classes? Read in our rooms with the dim
ceiling lights? Color with that basket of broken
crayons?
Play board games until one person
or another wandered off?

What we did, mostly,
was watch each other.
I watched the handsome man.

I watched him stand in line for his meds.
I watched him as he slumped on the little bench
by the Nurses' Station.

25

One day, I had a conversation with him. He said
he was undergoing daily shock treatments.
That's why he slept so much. He told me he heard
such treatments were 'The Gold Standard'
in care. I nodded, saying nothing
about what I knew of such things.
He seemed so hopeful.

I looked at his face, handsome
from a distance, but up close, those eyes. They
twirled
independent of each other. Ferris Wheels. A
glimpse
of the carnival in his head.

I pulled back. He was handsome again.
And he went back to bed.

Months later, I saw the handsome man again.
This time at an Outpatient Program.
Here, we were no longer locked up, deemed
'well enough' to leave each afternoon. But first,
we had to gather in a big room in a big circle, for
class.

Again, we learned to use our five senses, to count
colors. We learned that a bowl of ice cubes still
worked,
and how doing the dishes was a very good
distraction
from curling into a ball on the floor, screaming.

I raised my hand, said,

26

"I've lost everything. A normal daily
life, most of my friends, a career, my calling, my
income, my
memory. I have a Ph.D. and taught at a University
for 25 years, and here I am sitting
in this big circle of nothing, with nothing
ever changing. What am I
to expect?"

The Social Worker heading the class
nodded. Looked a little sad
on my behalf. She said
nothing.

Then we all slumped out to the sidewalk, to wait
for the little vans that took us
home. The handsome man approached me. Said
he was an engineer. He had an advanced
degree, had also taught at a University.
But every few years the sickness
returned, interrupted his traction.

So we had this in common. We both
were accomplished once. Had standing
in the community. We knew about
momentum, advancement. We had been
viable.

His eyes were calm when he
spoke. The carnival
in his head temporarily
closed. In its place, a keen
intelligence. Deep understanding.

27

The vans pulled up. He got in one. I got in another.
And we were carted home,
only to have the same thing
happen all over again the next day.

THE UNMARKED VAN

The routine was the same every day:
Drive to a nearby grocery store, park in the lot,
sit on the little bench and wait
for the unmarked van. The driver
was very nice, drove safely, his
big, retired-man hands firmly
on the wheel. He listened to
Big Band Swing turned down low.

After me, he would go to more
designated spots to pick up the others.
Like that guy at the edge of the road
by the apartment complex. He'd be smoking,
and he always looked like he was ready
to tie one on, be the life
of the party, but up close, he was
kind of sad. Slumped and furtive.

There was one pick-up that annoyed me.
We'd have to go out of our way to get a woman
right at her house. Why did she
get special treatment? The house
was old, a car needing repair,
was sinking slowly into her shabby yard.
How long had it been sinking like that?

See now, this was the summer I was meant
to rally. I would treat Outpatient like it was
my new profession, wearing the clothes I wore
when I still had a job, an official handbook
tidy in my lap, pen tucked
precisely into the spine.

Outpatient was different
from the main hospital, in its own building
at the base of the green lawn. The staff
were different, too. Not as good
as the nurses up the hill.
They kept their heads down during classes,
reading from notes, not noticing you even
if you were sobbing so hard your blouse
was sopped in tears and snot.

Even the driver of the unmarked van
would notice that much.

And so, even though
I got to dress up each morning, put on my face,
and listen to Sinatra for the half hour drive up I-87,
I thought, "Enough. This is just too lonely."

I went to my assigned therapist.
She had a nice office, comfortable sofas,
gentle paintings on mauve walls.
She was very efficient. Put together
like a job title. She was the perfect
brochure.

I dug out my heart,
cut it in two,
and slipped it
onto her tidy desk. It glistened
between us. I saw it. She didn't. I said,
"I don't want to be here anymore."
And she said, "Okay. We will sign you out."

And she reached into her close-to-empty
filing cabinet and pulled out
just the right form.
Just like that. So different
from the real hospital at the top of the hill.
They would never
let you out like that.

Later that day, I got in the unmarked van
for the last time. And the woman whose car
needed repair got in next to me.
Started talking.

"Do you live in in the town
where they drop me off? Near the grocery store?"
I said, "Yes," getting uneasy. Where
was this going? She asked, "What's
your name?" And already a boundary
was being crossed. She tore
a corner of a page from her handbook,
and gave it to me with a pen. She wanted
my full name, first and last. She wanted
my phone number. I gave her these things.
In return, she gave me her first name only,
and now I was nervous. See, I wasn't
crazy. I went to Outpatient because it was
my new job. But this woman next to me
might be crazy. Dangerous. And I never did put two
and two together that she and I
were in the same van and that my car might soon
be in need of repair, too.

THE LOBBY

The lobby of the Outpatient building
was quite pleasant.

It suggested visitors
with its upholstered chairs
and coffee table and magazines.
Although no one
really ever visited patients, there.

It suggested that one could come
and go as one pleased
with its pneumatic glass doors.
Although the staff would
run amok if you just
up and went.

In general, the lobby sat lifeless.
Big, airy, pristine, not
going anywhere. Never
looking any less new
than when it was
new.

Plus, it was air-conditioned.

When I was a patient there,
I would sit in the lobby near the magazines.
I would sit there a lot.

Each day, a young man,
let's call him Kevin, paced
back and forth, not speaking, just

staring straight ahead. Eventually,
he sat in one of the nice chairs
across from me.

Kevin was tall and scrawny, a bit
gallant. Easy to be around.
He didn't put up a fuss.

Sometimes a staffer
walked by, touched
his shoulder, asked,
"How are you doing, Kevin?"
And he'd look up and nod,
quiet and polite.

Then he'd go back
to staring straight ahead.

In this particular memory,
Kevin is clutching the arms of his chair.

What is going on in him
that he needs to gird himself, so?

What hauntings and agitations
are not tamped down
by the med cocktail he got
at the Main Hospital
before landing in Outpatient?

Is he seeing a demon
crouching in the chair
across from him, all fangs and slobber?

Is the room spinning so fast
around him, everything blurs
and runs together?

Is he hearing
voices the staffers
can't hear?
Are these voices singing? Speaking
in tongues? Is that demon
whispering falsehoods?

Does some pain pass through Kevin
so severe he feels the need
to upend the coffee table?
Punch an orderly? Punch himself?

In this particular memory,
Kevin is struggling to see
that it isn't real, whatever 'it'
might be, which torments him.

In this memory, Kevin is learning
to be, despite all reasons not to be,
kind. And gentle. And even
reassuring. So others around him
aren't scared
to be around him.

And I? Just what am I doing in the lobby?

Maybe I am coming to terms

with things this memory has
assigned to Kevin.

Maybe I am having flashbacks again.
Something is out
to destroy me. I need to flee.

Maybe I am unlatching
a trap door. Detaching
and rising upward, looking down
at the top of my head,
at my hollowed body folded
neatly in a chair. Numb.
Rabbit-dead.

And if a staffer were to touch my shoulder,
I, like Kevin, would somehow respond politely.

And this is where the memory ends.
This is where it drops us off:

A lobby like most others
where magazines rest unread
in a dazed woman's lap.
And a boy holds on
for dear life.

EPILOGUE

Years ago I had a cat that crawled under my bed covers and growled, as if it were being stalked and mauled by some external predator. After taking her to the vet, I learned that she had cancer. The predator was *inside* her.

For the longest time, I felt that situations outside myself caused me agony. Nobody understood me. Nobody was helping enough. Nobody cared enough. Nobody saw me. Nobody listened. Nobody was adept enough to pull me out from under the covers and quell my pain, like I wish I could have done for my little cat. The list of grievances was long: I was angry at my husband, my therapist, the pharmaceutical industry, the Patriarchy, insurance companies, my mother, the DSM, Emergency Room staffing, Social Security regulations, a cop or two, the entire psychiatric field, and my sorry ass life.

Was anger warranted? Oftentimes, yes. Absolutely. But I always slipped from anger into growling at what I perceived as external threats to my immediate safety. Growling is a knot of rage and terror. A matter of life and death. And I finally admit that I have diseases, including BiPolar I and PTSD, which are caused by faulty brain chemistry, old trauma, and genetics. The predators that make me growl are *inside* me. They have made me lose my sanity more than once and, during one harrowing night, they convinced me that the only redeeming thing to do was down a vial of sleeping pills during a barbecue. I have since spent a good deal of time training myself to sidestep a chute of negative messaging, which plummets straight into suicidal darkness. Have I resented the time I've poured into this self-training? Yes. Do I think it has been a waste of time? No. I am alive. And doing the best I have in years.

When I began writing *Hospital Poems*, I wasn't sure what would come out, what I had to say, what mattered most. I suspected that the poems would, at least somewhat, be an indictment of the medical establishment. But that didn't happen. My writing gravitated to my fellow patients. Their humanity. Their clumsiness and their grace as they took stock of their lives and navigated their illnesses. I have tremendous respect for all of them. And, in a number of patients I wrote about, I see pieces of me.

These poems, these patients, helped me to write my way out of the hospital.

For the reader who is suffering, I hope that my experiences can provide some comfort. If it's any consolation, I can say that I have made it, so far. No guarantees. No promises. No words of wisdom from someone who has been there and back. I very well might need the hospital again some day. The best I can offer is telling you that each person has something to share, which can resonate with someone else. Like the patients I met, whose stories were unique yet universal. Stories of despair balanced by hope; vulnerability balanced by strength. Each story can be of use in the telling. Mine included. And maybe yours, too.

So, what's your story?

ABOUT THE AUTHOR

Nancy Dunlop is a poet and essayist, who resides in Upstate New York. A finalist in the AWP Intro Journal Awards, she has been published in a number of print and digital journals, including *Swank*, *alterra*, *Truck*, *Green Kill Broad*sheet, *The Little Magazine*, *Writing on the Edge*, *13th Moon*, *Writers Resist: The Anthology*, and *Through the Looking Glass: Reflections on Madness and Chaos Within*. Her work has also been heard on NPR. She received her Ph.D. at UAlbany, SUNY, specializing in Creative Writing and Poetics. And she happily taught there, as well as other institutions, for 25 years. This is her first book.

Indie Blu(e) Publishing is a progressive, feminist micro-press, committed to producing honest and thought-provoking works. Our anthologies are meant to celebrate diversity and raise awareness. The editors all passionately advocate for human rights; mental health awareness; chronic illness awareness; sexual abuse survivors; and LGBTQ+ equality. It is our mission, and a great honor, to provide platforms for those voices that are stifled and stigmatized.

THROUGH THE LOOKING GLASS
REFLECTING ON MADNESS AND CHAOS WITHIN

An Indie Blu(e) Publishing Anthology

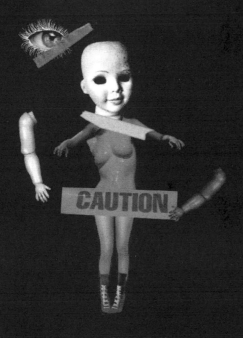

BUT YOU DON'T
LOOK SICK

The Real Life Adventures of Fibro Bitches, Lupus Warriors,
and other Superheroes Battling Invisible Illness

An Indie Blu(e) Publishing Anthology

WE ARE NOT OKAY

Elegy for a broken America
Memoir-in-essays

CHRISTIAN LIVERMORE

Made in the USA
Middletown, DE
23 September 2022

10846159R00043